Scroll Strong: A four week devotional for preteens exploring digital habits that honor God.

Published by: Nistel Press

Get more information at strongseriesdevos.com.

ISBN: 979-8-9921846-3-1

Printed in USA
First Edition 2025

a four week devotional
for preteens exploring
digital habits that
honor God.

by Joshua Celestin

START HERE

Welcome to a new book!

This is your book! Created just for you. Go ahead and write your name on the next page to make it yours.

We don't want you to just read this book but explore it.

Turn the page to see three ways to explore this book!

Signed,

- Joshua

THIS BOOK
BELONGS TO

three ways
to explore
this book

find an adult

Tell an adult that you are reading this book. Ask them to commit to discussing the questions with you after each day.

when you live with kindness, peace, & love to a world that needs it

how to use this book

read the day's Bible verse:
Begin by reading the selected verse together.

dive into the devotion:
Dive into the devotion inspired by the verse, exploring its meanings and applications.

discuss:
Discuss questions related to the verse and devotion, sharing insights and perspectives.

reflect:
Jot down thoughts, prayers, and reflections.

pray:
Read and connect with the prayer provided.

let's do it!

Whether you do one page a day, one page a week, or one page a month, these twenty days of devotionals will help you grow.

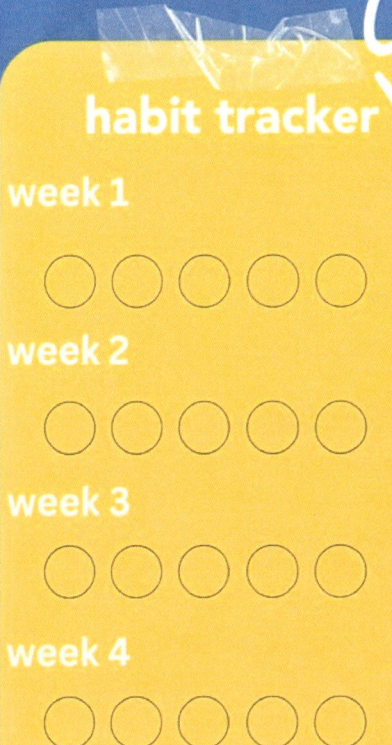

habit tracker

week 1

○ ○ ○ ○ ○

week 2

○ ○ ○ ○ ○

week 3

○ ○ ○ ○ ○

week 4

○ ○ ○ ○ ○

week 1
verses

Day 1: You Are More Than Your Profile
Psalm 139:13-14 (NIV)
"I praise you because I am
fearfully and wonderfully made..."

Day 2: The Highlights vs. The Whole Story
1 Samuel 16:7 (NIV)
"People look at the outward appearance,
but the Lord looks at the heart."

Day 3: Screen Time vs. Soul Time
Matthew 6:33 (NIV)
"But seek first his kingdom and his righteousness..."

Day 4: Likes Don't Define You
Galatians 1:10 (NIV)
"Am I now trying to win the approval
of human beings, or of God?"

Day 5: Set Up Guardrails
Proverbs 4:23 (NIV)
"Above all else, guard your heart,
for everything you do flows from it."

who am I online?

week 2

verses

Day 1: What You See Shapes You
Philippians 4:8 (NIV)
"Whatever is true, whatever is noble, whatever is right,
whatever is pure... think about such things."

Day 2: Not Everything Online Is True
Proverbs 14:15 (NIV)
"The simple believe anything,
but the prudent give thought to their steps."

Day 3: Temptation in One Click
1 Corinthians 10:13 (NIV)
"God is faithful; he will not let you be
tempted beyond what you can bear."

Day 4: Who's Influencing You?
Proverbs 13:20 (NIV)
"Walk with the wise and become wise,
for a companion of fools suffers harm."

Day 5: Click Wisely, Live Wisely
Ephesians 5:15-16 (NIV)
"Be very careful, then, how you live—not as unwise
but as wise, making the most of every opportunity..."

what should i click on?

week 3

verses

Day 1: Words Have Power
Proverbs 18:21 (NIV)
"The tongue has the power of life and death..."

Day 2: Think Before You Post
James 1:19 (NIV)
"Everyone should be quick to listen,
slow to speak and slow to become angry."

Day 3: No Room for Hate
Ephesians 4:29 (NIV)
"Do not let any unwholesome talk come out of your mouths,
but only what is helpful for building others up..."

Day 4: What to Do About Cyberbullying
Romans 12:17 (NIV)
"Do not repay anyone evil for evil.
Be careful to do what is right in the eyes of everyone."

Day 5: Use Your Words for Good
Matthew 5:16 (NIV)
"Let your light shine before others,
that they may see your good deeds
and glorify your Father in heaven."

how do I talk online?

week 4

verses

Day 1: Your Online Life Is Part of Your Faith
Colossians 3:17 (NIV)
"And whatever you do, whether in word or deed,
do it all in the name of the Lord Jesus..."

Day 2: Encourage One Another
1 Thessalonians 5:11 (NIV)
"Encourage one another and build each other up..."

Day 3: Share Your Faith Without Being Weird
Matthew 5:14 (NIV)
"You are the light of the world.
A town built on a hill cannot be hidden."

Day 4: Use Technology to Grow Closer to God
Psalm 119:105 (NIV)
"Your word is a lamp for my feet,
a light on my path."

Day 5: Make a Difference Online and Offline
James 1:22 (NIV)
"Do not merely listen to the word,
and so deceive yourselves. Do what it says."

how can I honor God online?

When you live with kindness, peace, & love to a world that needs it.

Kindness

"When you live with kindness, truth, and love,
you are shining the light of Jesus
to a world that needs it!"

table of contents

week

who am i
online?

week one

who am i online?

introduction

Have you ever felt like you had to prove yourself to be liked or noticed? This week we're talking all about that! We'll explore how your value doesn't come from likes, followers, or attention. It comes from who God made you to be. You'll learn why you don't have to compare yourself to others, how to put God first, and how to protect your heart in a world that sometimes gets it all mixed up. Get ready to discover how God sees you and why that's the best news ever!

overview

1. day one: more than your profile — **Psalm 139:13-14**
2. day two: the highlights vs. the whole story — **1 Samuel 16:7**
3. day three: screen time vs. soul time — **Matthew 6:33**
4. day four: likes don't define you — **Galatians 1:10**
5. day five: set up guardrails — **Proverbs 4:23**

more than your profile.

Read: Psalm 139:13-14

Have you ever wanted to impress someone by showing off something cool about yourself?

What was it? Write it down!

```



```

It feels good to be noticed, right? It feels good when people give us a thumbs-up, cheer for us, or say "good job!"

And when you get older and start using things like phones, screens, or social media, you'll see that people often try to show their best selves online through cool pictures, fun videos, and exciting updates.

But here's the truth: **your value isn't in your profile, your bio, or even your username.** It's in who God made you to be!

The Bible reminds us in Psalm 139 that we are "fearfully and wonderfully made." That means God made you with great care and attention. He loves you so much, no matter what you post (or don't post) online.

Even if you're not online yet, you're already building your identity. God's view of you never changes based on likes or followers.

Three Ways to Live This Out:

1. *Remember What God Says About You* — When you see someone get lots of likes, remember: God already calls you wonderfully made. That matters most!

2. *Celebrate Others Without Comparing* — Cheer for your friends wins without feeling like you have to compete. You're already valuable to God.

3. *Talk to Someone About This* — Ask a parent or leader how they handle online pressure.

what's next

discussion questions

1. What are some things you're really proud of about yourself?
2. How do you think God sees you, even if you never post anything online?
3. Why is it important to remember that our identity comes from God and not from likes and comments?

let's pray

Dear God, thank You for making me in a wonderful way. Help me remember that my value doesn't come from what others think or say about me, but from who You say I am. Teach me to see myself the way You see me. In Jesus name, we pray. Amen.

You're more than your profile.

notes

today i'm grateful for:

1.

2.

3.

today i learned that:

my thoughts for the day:

Day 2

the highlights vs. the whole story.

Read: 1 Samuel 16:7

Have you ever seen a picture of someone having fun and thought, "Wow, I wish I was doing that!" Maybe it was a vacation, a party, or something else exciting.

When you see pictures or videos online, or on YouTube, it's easy to think that everyone else is always having fun. Their lives look so perfect! But here's something you should know: most people only post their best moments online.

It's like showing a highlight reel. They share the cool things like winning a game, going to a fun place, or hanging out with friends.

What you *don't* see is everything else: the times they felt left out, made a mistake, or had a boring day.

The Bible says in 1 Samuel 16:7, "People look at the outward appearance, but the Lord looks at the heart."

That means God sees way more than just the fun photos or videos. He knows the whole story of your life. Even the parts you don't share with anyone else!

When ever you start using the internet or see what others post, remember: **God knows your whole story, and He cares about every part of it.**

You don't have to compare your behind-the-scenes to someone else's highlight reel. God sees you, knows you, and loves you just as you are!

How to Focus on the Whole Story:

1. *Be Honest With Yourself* — Remember that what you see online is not the full story. Everyone has ups and downs!

2. *Thank God For Your Story* — Even if it doesn't feel exciting all the time, your story matters to God.

3. *Celebrate Real Moments* — Enjoy the small everyday moments in your life.

what's next

discussion questions

1. Has there ever been a time when something looked exciting or fun, but deep down, you knew there was more going on behind the scenes?
2. What makes it tough to remember that what we see online is just the highlights?
3. How does it make you feel to know that God sees and cares about your whole story?

let's pray

Dear God, thank You for knowing my whole story. The good parts and the hard parts. Help me not to compare my life to what I see online. Help me to trust that You care about every part of my life. In Jesus name, we pray. Amen.

God knows your whole story.

today i'm grateful for:

1. _____

2. _____

3. _____

today i learned that: _____

_____

_____

_____

my thoughts for the day: _____

_____

_____

_____

screen time vs. soul time.

Read: Matthew 6:33

Have you ever been so into a game or show that you didn't want to stop, even when it was time for something else?

What was it?

Screens can be so fun. Whether it's playing games, watching videos, or scrolling through funny pictures, it's easy to get caught up and lose track of time. Before you know it, an hour (or more!) has gone by.

Now, there's nothing wrong with having fun online or with games.

But here's something important to remember: **what you spend time on shapes your heart.**

Matthew 6:33 says, *"But seek first His kingdom and His righteousness..."* That means we should put God first. Before screens, games, or anything else.

When we spend time with God by reading the Bible, praying, or just thinking about Him, we grow closer to Him. And when we do that, everything else in life starts to make more sense!

Choosing Soul Time Over Screen Time:

1. *Start Your Day With God* — Before you grab your tablet or turn on the TV, say a quick prayer to God or think about something you're thankful for.

2. *Swap Screen Time for Scripture* — If you normally play a game or watch a show at a certain time, try reading a Bible verse instead once this week!

3. *All About Balance* — If you've been on a screen for a while, take a break! Do something that helps you grow closer to God or to others.

what's next

discussion questions

1. What are some fun things you like to do on your screens? What are some fun things you like to do off of them?
2. Screens are fun and easy to use, but how can we still make sure God comes first?
3. Why do you think spending time with God is important for your heart and your choices?

let's pray

Dear God, thank You for all the fun things I get to do. Help me to remember to put You first every day. Show me how to balance my time so that I grow closer to You. In Jesus name, we pray. Amen.

what you spend time on shapes your heart.

today i'm grateful for:

1. _____

2. _____

3. _____

today i learned that: _____

_____

_____

_____

my thoughts for the day: _____

_____

_____

_____

likes don't define you.

Read: Galatians 1:10

Have you ever done something just to get noticed? Maybe you told a funny joke, wore your favorite outfit, or showed off something cool?

Write it down!

It feels good when people recognize us.

That's why, when people start using things like social media or games online, they sometimes try really hard to get likes, comments, or high scores to get people to notice them.

But here's something important to remember: **likes don't define you.** Even if one person or a million people see your post, or YouTube video, God's love stays the same.

Galatians 1:10 asks, *"Am I now trying to win the approval of human beings, or of God?"*

Even if you're not online much yet, this is good to know now! The online world might try to tell you that your value comes from numbers and attention. But God already says you're valuable because He made you and loves you.

Focusing on God's Approval, Not Likes:

1. *Think About What Makes God Proud* — When you're about to share something, ask yourself: "Is this showing kindness, love, or truth?"

2. *Remember Your Worth Is Already Set* — Whether people notice or not, you are fully loved by God.

3. *Encourage Someone Else* — Instead of waiting for likes, go give some encouragement!

what's next

discussion questions

1. How do you feel when people like or comment on something you do?
2. Why is it better to focus on God's love instead of people's approval?
3. What are some ways we can remind ourselves that God's love never changes?

let's pray

Dear God, it feels good when people notice me, but I know Your love matters most. Help me not to chase after likes or approval from others. Teach me to care most about what You think. In Jesus name, we pray. Amen.

likes don't
define you.

today i'm grateful for:

1. _____

2. _____

3. _____

today i learned that: _____

_____

_____

_____

my thoughts for the day: _____

_____

_____

_____

set up guardrails.

Read: Proverbs 4:23

Have you ever seen guardrails on a road? Maybe on a bridge or a sharp curve? Guardrails are there to keep cars safe.

They help drivers stay on the right path and keep them from going into dangerous places.

We need guardrails in our lives, too. Especially when it comes to how we use the internet, games, or even screen time.

The Bible tells us in Proverbs 4:23, "*Above all else, guard your heart, for everything you do flows from it.*"

Your heart is special. It's where your thoughts, choices, and feelings start.

If you want to make wise choices online and in life, you need to protect your heart by setting up some boundaries.

That could mean having limits for how long you play games, what kinds of videos you watch, or even asking a parent before you go on certain websites.

These guardrails help keep you safe, help you honor God, and make sure you're choosing things that are good for your heart and mind.

Building Good Guardrails:

1. *Decide Your Limits Early* — Think about how much time feels healthy for online and talk about it with your parents.

2. *Choose Good Content* — Pick shows, games, and videos that are fun but also honor God and help you grow.

3. *Ask For Help* — If you're not sure if something is safe or good, ask a trusted adult! Guardrails work best when we build them together.

what's next

discussion questions

1. Why do you think it's smart to have guardrails (limits) for screens and online use?
2. What are some good rules we can make for using screens?
3. How can guardrails help protect your heart and your choices?

let's pray

Dear God, thank You for giving me the wisdom to make good choices. Help me set up guardrails that keep my heart safe. Show me the best way to use my time and my technology to honor You. In Jesus name, we pray. Amen.

set up your guardrails.

today i'm grateful for:

1. _____

2. _____

3. _____

today i learned that: _____

_____

_____

_____

my thoughts for the day: _____

_____

_____

_____

week

what
should i
click on?

week two

what should i click on?

introduction

Have you ever noticed how some things you watch or hear stay stuck in your mind all day? This week we're talking about why that happens and why it matters! We'll learn how what we watch, click, and listen to shapes our hearts, our minds, and even our choices. You'll discover how to fill your mind with good things, how to tell what's true online, and how to make wise choices with every click. Get ready to learn how to protect your heart, build good habits, and grow into the person God made you to be!

overview

1. day one: what you see shapes you — **Philippians 4:8**
2. day two: not everything online is true — **Proverbs 14:15**
3. day three: temptation in one click — **1 Corinthians 10:13**
4. day four: who's influencing you — **Proverbs 13:20**
5. day five: click and live wisely — **Ephesians 5:15-16**

Day 1

what you see shapes you.

Read: Philippians 4:8

Have you ever watched or read something that stuck in your mind all day? Maybe a funny video, a cool story, or even words that you shouldn't say?

What was it?

The things we see and hear can stay in our minds for a long time. Maybe you've noticed this with songs, videos, or even conversations. Sometimes, something silly can make you laugh all day. Other times, something not-so-good can make you feel worried or upset, even after you've stopped watching.

That's because **what we see shapes us.** It shapes the way we think, the way we talk, and even the choices we make.

That's why the Bible tells us in Philippians 4:8 to think about things that are true, noble, right, and pure. In other words, things that help us grow in the right way!

The online world is full of choices. Videos to watch. People to follow. Games to play.

But not everything is helpful for your heart and mind.

Making Strong Choices About What You Watch:

1. *Think Before You Click* — Ask yourself: "Will this help me think about good things?"
2. *Choose Good Influences* — Follow people and watch videos that encourage you, not ones that fill your mind with stuff that feels wrong or doesn't honor God.
3. *Talk It Out* — If you're not sure about something, ask a parent or leader for help before you click.

what's next

discussion questions

1. Can you think of something you saw or heard recently that stuck in your mind? Why do you think it stuck with you?
2. Why is it important to choose to watch or listen to things that are good for your heart and mind?
3. How can we make sure we're filling our minds with good and helpful things?

let's pray

Dear God, thank You for giving me so many choices about what to watch and listen to. Help me choose things that fill my heart and mind with what is true, good, and right. Help me grow closer to You with every choice I make. In Jesus name, we pray. Amen.

what you see shapes you.

notes

today i'm grateful for:

1.

2.

3.

today i learned that:

my thoughts for the day:

not everything online is true.

Read: Proverbs 14:15

Have you ever heard something that sounded true but later found out it wasn't? Maybe it was a story or a crazy fact that turned out to be wrong.

The internet is full of information. Some of it is helpful, and some of it is just plain wrong!

Maybe you've seen a video that says something unbelievable or read a headline that makes you stop and wonder if it's true.

The truth is, **not everything online is true.**

That's why the Bible gives us wise advice in Proverbs 14:15. It says, *"The simple believe anything, but the prudent give thought to their steps."*

In other words, wise people don't just believe everything they hear or see. They stop and think about it first!

Even if you're not online much yet, this is important to remember. Someday soon, you'll be choosing what to click, watch, and believe. And you can be ready! When you hear something surprising, or even a little suspicious, pause and think before you believe it or share it with someone else.

Being wise with what you believe online helps protect your heart and your mind, and it helps you share truth with others too!

Being Wise About What You Believe Online:

1. *Pause Before You Believe* — Just because it's on the internet doesn't mean it's true!

2. *Check With a Trusted Adult* — If you're not sure something is true, ask a parent or leader to help you figure it out.

3. *Think Before You Share* — Before you tell someone else, make sure what you're sharing is actually true and helpful!

what's next

discussion questions

1. Have you ever believed something that turned out to be untrue? How did that feel?
2. Why is it important to think carefully before we believe or share something online?
3. What are some ways we can tell if something online is true or not?

let's pray

Dear God, help me to be wise when I'm online. Teach me to stop and think before I believe or share something. Help me to love truth and make choices that honor You. In Jesus name, we pray. Amen.

not everything online is true.

today i'm grateful for:

1. _____

2. _____

3. _____

today i learned that: _____

_____

_____

_____

my thoughts for the day: _____

_____

_____

_____

temptation in one click.

Read: 1 Corinthians 10:13

Have you ever felt tempted to do something you knew wasn't the best choice? Maybe it was sneaking an extra snack or saying something rude when you were upset.

Write it down!

```

```

Temptation is a tricky thing. It's that feeling inside when you know something isn't right, but it still looks fun or exciting.

Online, temptation can happen with just **one click.** Watching a video you know you shouldn't, playing a game when you were supposed to be doing something else, or making a social media account even when your parents said you couldn't.

Here's the good news: **you're not alone in this.**

The Bible says in 1 Corinthians 10:13, *"God is faithful; he will not let you be tempted beyond what you can bear."*

That means even when you feel tempted, God gives you the strength to say no.

Learning to spot temptation early will help you grow stronger and make choices that protect your heart and honor God.

How to Handle Online Temptation:

1. *Stop and Think First* — Before you click, ask: "Is this a good choice? Would this make God proud?"

2. *Remind Yourself of What's True* — When you feel tempted, say to yourself: "God help me make wise choices!"

3. *Choose to Walk Away* — If you spot something tempting, remember you don't have to click. You have the power to walk away!

what's next

discussion questions

1. What are some examples of things online that might be tempting but not helpful?
2. Why is it a good idea to pause and think before clicking on something?
3. How can we remind ourselves to make good choices when we feel tempted online?

let's pray

Dear God, thank You for helping me when I feel tempted. Please give me the strength to make wise choices, even when it's hard. Help me remember that You are always with me, giving me the power to do what's right. In Jesus name, we pray. Amen.

you're not alone in this.

notes

today i'm grateful for:

1. _____

2. _____

3. _____

today i learned that: _____

_____

_____

_____

my thoughts for the day: _____

_____

_____

_____

Day 4

who's influencing you?

Read: Proverbs 13:20

Who is someone you look up to? Maybe it's a teacher, a coach, a family member, or even someone you've seen online.

The people we look up to have a big influence on us. We often start to think, act, and talk like them without even realizing it!

This happens with people we know in real life, but also with the people we follow or watch online.

That's why the Bible gives us great advice in Proverbs 13:20: *"Walk with the wise and become wise, for a companion of fools suffers harm."* In simple words, it means if you spend time with wise people, you'll become wise too. But if you follow people who make foolish choices, it can lead you in the wrong direction.

Whenever you do get the chance to watch videos, play games, or follow others online, choose people who make good choices, speak kindly, and encourage you to be your best.

Your attention is valuable. So give it to people who help you grow closer to God!

Choosing Wise Influences:

1. *Notice How They Make You Feel* — After you watch or follow someone, ask yourself: "Do they make me want to be more like Jesus?

2. *Pick People Who Lift You Up* — Follow people who encourage you to do the right thing, not ones who make fun of others.

3. *Remember You Can Unfollow* — If someone is not a good influence, it's okay to stop watching or following them. Protect your heart!

what's next

discussion questions

1. Who are some people you think are good influences? Why do they stand out to you?
2. What kinds of things should we look for when we choose who to follow or watch?
3. How does spending time with wise people help us make better choices?

let's pray

Dear God, thank You for the people who encourage me to do what's right. Help me to choose good influences, both in real life and online. Show me how to follow people who help me grow closer to You. In Jesus name, we pray. Amen.

your attention is valuable.

today i'm grateful for:

1. _____

2. _____

3. _____

today i learned that: _____

_____

_____

_____

my thoughts for the day: _____

_____

_____

_____

Day 5

click and live wisely.

Read: Ephesians 5:15-16

Have you ever made a small choice that led to something big? Maybe you practiced a little every day and got really good at something!

Small choices might not seem like a big deal at the time, but they really add up. Think about this. Brushing your teeth every day keeps them healthy. Practicing your spelling words helps you do better on tests. Little things matter!

The same is true with what you click on or watch online.

Every time you choose what to click, you're actually building a habit. Watching one good video might not change everything, but watching good, wise things over and over will help your heart and mind grow stronger.

The Bible reminds us in Ephesians 5:15-16 to "be very careful, then, how you live—not as unwise but as wise, making the most of every opportunity."

That means we should pay attention to our choices, even the small ones, because they shape who we become.

Whether you're already online a lot or not much yet, this is the perfect time to start building smart habits. When you learn to click wisely, you're learning to live wisely too!

Building Good Clicking Habits:
1. *Think About Where It Leads* — Before you click, ask: "Will this help me grow in the right direction?"
2. *Pick Positive Patterns* — Keep choosing good things online, even when no one else is watching.
3. *Remember: Small Choices Add Up* — Little by little, wise choices shape who you become.

what's next

discussion questions

1. Why do you think small choices online are so important?
2. Can you think of a time when a small choice turned into a good habit?
3. How can we build wise habits when it comes to what we watch, play, and click?

let's pray

Dear God, help me to remember that every click and choice matters. Teach me to use my time and my choices to grow stronger in You. Thank You for helping me build wise habits that honor You every day. In Jesus name, we pray. Amen.

choices shape who we become.

today i'm grateful for:

1. _____

2. _____

3. _____

today i learned that: _____

_____

_____

_____

my thoughts for the day: _____

_____

_____

_____

week

how do i talk online?

week three

how do i talk online?

introduction

Have you ever had someone say something that made your whole day better? This week we're talking about how powerful words really are! We'll learn why what we say matters, how to think before we speak or post, and how to use our words to bring light instead of hurt. You'll discover how to stand up against negativity, build others up, and shine with kindness both online and in real life. Get ready to find out how your words can make a big difference!

overview

1. day one: words have power — **Proverbs 18:21**
2. day two: think before you post — **James 1:19**
3. day three: no room for hate — **Ephesians 4:29**
4. day four: what to do about cyberbullying — **Romans 12:17**
5. day five: use your words for good — **Matthew 5:16**

Day 1

words have power.

Read: Proverbs 18:21

Has someone ever said something to you that made you feel really good?

What did they say?

```



```

Words are powerful! Just a few words can make you feel excited and confident.

But words can also hurt. Maybe you've heard someone say something unkind or mean. That can really not sit well with you.

The Bible says in Proverbs 18:21, *"The tongue has the power of life and death."*

That means our words can either lift people up or tear them down. And guess what? This is true not just when we speak out loud, but also when we write texts, leave comments, or play games online.

You get to decide. Will your words be used to build others up, or tear them down? When you choose to encourage, celebrate, and speak kindly; you're using the power of your words in a way that honors God and helps others feel seen and loved.

Using Words to Build Up:

1. *Think Before You Type* — Before you send a message or comment, ask: "Will this build someone up?"

2. *Be an Encourager* — Look for a chance to cheer someone on today.

3. *Walk Away From Mean Words* — If you see mean comments or messages, choose not to join in. Use your words for good!

what's next

discussion questions

1. Can you think of a time when someone's kind words made you feel great? What did they say?
2. Why do you think words can be so powerful, even if they're just a short message or comment?
3. What's one way you can use your words to build someone up today?

let's pray

Dear God, thank You for the power of words. Help me to choose words that build people up and show Your love. Teach me to think before I speak or type, and to always use my words for good. In Jesus name, we pray. Amen.

words have power.

today i'm grateful for:

1. _____

2. _____

3. _____

today i learned that: _____

_____

_____

_____

my thoughts for the day: _____

_____

_____

_____

Day 2

think before you post.

Read: James 1:19

Have you ever said something quickly and then wished you could take it back?

What happened?

[ ]

Sometimes, when we're upset or excited, words can come out fast! That happens in real life, but it also happens online.

Maybe you feel like replying to a comment really quickly, or you want to post something the moment you think of it.

But once you post or send something, you can't take it back. It's out there!

That's why the Bible gives us wise advice in James 1:19: *"Everyone should be quick to listen, slow to speak and slow to become angry."*

This means before we say (or type) anything, we should slow down, take a breath, and think first.

Your words have power, and your choice to pause can make a big difference!

Smart Posting Habits:

1. *Pause Before You Post* — Ask yourself: "Is this helpful, kind, and true?"

2. *Cool Down First* — If you're upset, wait until you're calm before saying or posting anything.

3. *Remember It Lasts* — Once you post something, it stays. Make sure it's something you'll be proud of later!

what's next

discussion questions

1. Why do you think it's important to pause before we say or post something?
2. How could waiting a moment before posting help us make better choices online?
3. What's a helpful question you can ask yourself before you post or send a message?

let's pray

Dear God, sometimes it's easy to say or post things quickly without thinking. Help me to pause, to be wise, and to use my words carefully. In Jesus name, we pray. Amen.

think before you post.

today i'm grateful for:

1. _____

2. _____

3. _____

today i learned that: _____

_____

_____

_____

my thoughts for the day: _____

_____

_____

_____

no room for hate.

Read: Ephesians 4:29

Have you ever heard someone say something mean, either in person or online?

How did it make you feel when you heard it?

Maybe you've seen people leave mean comments online or make fun of someone in a group chat or game. It can happen so fast!

People might even try to be funny by being sarcastic or teasing someone else, but instead of making people laugh, it leaves someone feeling hurt.

That's not what God wants for us.

The Bible says in Ephesians 4:29, *"Do not let any unwholesome talk come out of your mouths, but only what is helpful for building others up."*

God wants us to use our words to build people up, not tear them down!

When we use our words to encourage others, we make the spaces we're in so much better. Let's choose words that help others feel loved, noticed, and valued. There's no room for hate when we're following God's way!

Choosing Words That Build Up:

1. *Leave Kind Comments* — If you say something online, make sure it's kind and encouraging!

2. *Ignore the Negativity* — If you see mean or hurtful comments, don't join in. Walk away from the hate.

3. *Be the Positive Voice* — Look for ways to cheer someone up with your words today, whether in person or online!

what's next

discussion questions

1. Have you ever seen someone being mean online? How did that make you feel?
2. What are some better choices we can make when we see negativity or unkind comments?
3. How can you be a positive voice in places where others are being hurtful?

let's pray

Dear God, help me to choose kindness, even when it feels easier to be negative or mean. Show me how to be a voice of love and hope, both in person and online. Let my words make a difference for good. In Jesus name, we pray. Amen.

there is
no room for hate.

today i'm grateful for:

1. _____

2. _____

3. _____

today i learned that: _____

_____

_____

_____

my thoughts for the day: _____

_____

_____

_____

what to do about cyberbullying.

Read: Romans 12:17

Have you ever seen or heard about someone being bullied? Maybe it was at school, on a team, or even online.

Seeing or hearing about bullying is never easy.

And now, because of the internet, bullying doesn't just happen at school or on the playground. It can also happen in texts, in games, or on social media. That's called **cyberbullying.**

Cyberbullying is when someone uses words or pictures online to hurt, tease, or embarrass someone else.

The Bible teaches us in Romans 12:17:
"Do not repay anyone evil for evil. Be careful to do what is right in the eyes of everyone."

That means even if someone is being unkind or hurtful, we don't respond by being mean back. Instead, we do what is right.

So, what can you do if you see cyberbullying?

Even if you're not online much yet, you can start practicing these choices now.

You can refuse to join in, and if you feel unsure, you can tell a trusted adult who can help. Remember: you have the power to make a difference!

Responding to Cyberbullying the Right Way:

1. *Don't Join In* — Even if others are teasing or being mean, choose not to add to it.

2. *Speak Up with Kindness* — If it's safe, say something kind to the person being hurt. A kind word can make a difference!

3. *Get Help When Needed* — If you see bullying online, tell a trusted adult so they can help stop it.

what's next

discussion questions

1. What should we do if you see someone being bullied online?
2. Why is it important not to respond to unkindness with more unkindness?
3. What are some ways you can help someone who's being bullied feel supported?

let's pray

Dear God, help me to be brave and kind when I see bullying. Show me how to use my words to help others and not to hurt. Give me wisdom to know what to do, and the courage to do what is right. In Jesus name, we pray. Amen.

you have the power to make a difference.

today i'm grateful for:

1. _____

2. _____

3. _____

today i learned that: _____

_____

_____

_____

my thoughts for the day: _____

_____

_____

_____

use your words for good.

Read: Matthew 5:16

Have you ever seen someone do something that made others smile or feel better?

Kindness stands out. When someone helps, shares, or encourages others, it's like they're shining a bright light in a dark place.

The internet is full of all kinds of things—some good, and some not so good. But here's the good thing: **you can be a bright light online too!**

You can use your words in chats, comments, or messages to encourage and show people what it looks like to follow Jesus.

Jesus said in Matthew 5:16, *"Let your light shine before others, that they may see your good deeds and glorify your Father in heaven."* That means your words and actions can help others see God's love!

Even if you're not online much yet, you can start practicing now by using your words for good wherever you are.

That way, when you do get the chance to be online, you'll already be ready to shine bright!

Shining Bright with Your Words:

1. *Share Encouraging Words* — Say things that will build people up.

2. *Be a Light in Dark Spaces* — If you notice a space (online or in real life) where people are being mean, choose to bring kindness instead.

3. *Celebrate Others* — Cheer for your friends successes! A kind comment or message can brighten someone's whole day.

what's next

discussion questions

1. How can you let your light shine with your words, both online and in real life?
2. What's one encouraging thing you could say to a friend today?
3. Why do you think God wants us to use our words to help others see His love?

let's pray

Dear God, thank You for giving me the chance to shine Your light with my words. Help me to encourage others and to use my words to point people to You. Let my words bring joy and hope to everyone I meet. In Jesus name, we pray. Amen.

use your words for good.

today i'm grateful for:

1. _____

2. _____

3. _____

today i learned that: _____

_____

_____

_____

my thoughts for the day: _____

_____

_____

_____

week

how can i honor God online?

week four

how can i honor God online?

introduction

Have you ever been part of something that made you feel proud and excited to show up and give it your best? This week we are talking about how your online life is part of your faith too. We will learn how everything we do, what we say, what we post, and even what we click, can show others who Jesus is. You will find out how to encourage others, share your faith naturally, use technology to grow closer to God, and make a real difference both online and offline.

overview

1. day one: online life is part of your faith — **Colossians 3:17**
2. day two: encourage one another — **1 Thessalonians 5:11**
3. day three: share your faith — **Matthew 5:14**
4. day four: use tech to grow closer to God — **Psalm 119:105**
5. day five: make a difference anywhere — **James 1:22**

Day 1

online life is part of your faith.

Read: Colossians 3:17

Have you ever been part of something that made you feel really proud? Maybe a team, a school project, or helping with something important.

When you're part of something you're proud of, you want to give it your best, right?

Maybe you wear your team shirt, show up on time, and play hard. You know you're representing your team, so you want to do it well!

Guess what? **Being a follower of Jesus is like that too.**

No matter where you are, whether you're at school, at home, or even online, you represent Jesus.

Colossians 3:17 says, *"And whatever you do, whether in word or deed, do it all in the name of the Lord Jesus."*

That means everything we do, even the way we use technology, is a way to show people who Jesus is.

When you play a game online or comment on a video, you have a choice.

Will you use your words and actions to reflect Jesus?

Whether in person or online, your faith isn't just for Sundays, it's for every day!

Living Out Your Faith Online:

1. *Choose Words That Honor Jesus* — Before you type or click, think: "Does this show God's love?"
2. *Play and Post With Intention* — Whether it's in a game or a comment, use your actions to encourage others.
3. *Remember You Represent Jesus* — Every space you're in, online or not, is a chance to show who you follow!

what's next

discussion questions

1. What are some ways you can show your faith in everyday life, not just at church?
2. How can the way you act online show people that you follow Jesus?
3. Why do you think it matters to represent Jesus in everything you do, including using technology?

let's pray

Dear God, thank You for reminding me that my whole life belongs to You, both online and offline. Help me make choices that show others who You are. Teach me to honor You with everything I do and say. In Jesus name, we pray. Amen.

you represent Jesus.

today i'm grateful for:

1. _____

2. _____

3. _____

today i learned that: _____

_____

_____

_____

my thoughts for the day: _____

_____

_____

_____

encourage one another.

Read: 1 Thessalonians 5:11

Have you ever had someone cheer you on or say something nice that made your day better?

CIRCLE ONE: YES OR NO

It feels really good when someone encourages us. A kind word, a high-five, or a simple "You've got this!" can make a huge difference.

Now think about this. When you're online, are you just looking at things, or are you also using that time to encourage others?

It's easy to scroll, watch, or play and forget that the internet is more than just a place to consume things. It's also a place where you can **contribute and encourage others.**

The Bible says in 1 Thessalonians 5:11, *"Encourage one another and build each other up."*

That means we should look for ways to lift people up, even online!

Using the Internet to Build Others Up:

1. *Leave a Kind Comment* — Cheer someone on in a game or say something encouraging in a chat.

2. *Share Good Stuff* — If you see something positive and kind, share it with others to brighten their day!

3. *Look for Ways to Lift Others* — Every time you're online, ask yourself: "Who can I encourage today?"

what's next

discussion questions

1. Have you ever sent or received an encouraging message? How did it make you feel?
2. What are some ways you can spread kindness online, even with a small comment or post?
3. How can you remember to use the internet for encouragement, not just entertainment?

let's pray

Dear God, thank You for giving me the chance to encourage others. Help me to use my words online to build people up and spread kindness. Show me small ways I can make a big difference. In Jesus name, we pray. Amen.

contribute and encourage others.

today i'm grateful for:

1. _____

2. _____

3. _____

today i learned that: _____

_____

_____

_____

my thoughts for the day: _____

_____

_____

_____

Day 3

share your faith.

Read: Matthew 5:14

Have you ever seen someone do something brave and kind in front of others?

What did they do?

Sometimes, it can feel a little awkward to share your faith. You might think, *"What if people think I'm weird?"* or *"What if they don't listen?"*

Especially online, it's easy to feel unsure about how to show you love Jesus without feeling like you're trying too hard.

But here's the good news: you don't have to preach a big message or write super long posts to share your faith!

Jesus said in Matthew 5:14, *"You are the light of the world. A town built on a hill cannot be hidden."*

When you follow Jesus, your actions and words already shine bright! While that's not all we're called to do, living this way can open the door to even more meaningful conversations. And when we do get the chance to share our faith, we should. There's no reason to feel awkward about it.

When you live like Jesus, people will notice, and your light will shine for God!

Shining Bright Without Being Weird:

1. *Show Love in Simple Ways* — Be kind and respectful in your posts and comments.
2. *Share Good Things* — Post Bible verses, songs, or stories that encourage others.
3. *Let Your Actions Speak* — How you treat people online shows what you believe. Let your actions shine!

what's next

discussion questions

1. What are some natural ways to show people you follow Jesus without feeling awkward?
2. Why is it important to let your actions show your faith, not just your words?
3. Have you ever seen someone do something that showed they believed in God? What did they do?

let's pray

Dear God, help me to shine Your light wherever I go. Give me courage to show my faith in a way that feels natural and real. Let my actions and words point others to You, both online and in real life. In Jesus name, we pray. Amen.

share your light.

today i'm grateful for:

1. _____

2. _____

3. _____

today i learned that: _____

_____

_____

_____

my thoughts for the day: _____

_____

_____

_____

use tech to grow closer to God.

Read: Psalm 119:105

Have you ever used a flashlight in the dark?

When you're in the dark, even a small light can make a huge difference. It helps you see where you're going so you don't trip or get lost!

The Bible is like that flashlight. Psalm 119:105 says, *"Your word is a lamp for my feet, a light on my path."*

It helps us see what's right and shows us the way to go. And here's something really cool: technology can actually help you keep that light shining bright!

It's easy to think of technology as a distraction, but you can use it to grow closer to God too.

There are Bible apps that let you read and listen to God's Word, worship playlists to help you praise Him, and videos that teach you more about who God is.

Even if you don't have your own phone yet, you can ask a parent to explore these tools together.

When you use technology in the right way, it can actually help you walk closer with God every day!

Ways to Use Technology to Grow With God:

1. *Listen to Worship Music* — Play songs that help you focus on God's love.

2. *Explore a Bible App* — Use a Bible app to read or listen to Scripture, even for just a few minutes a day.

3. *Watch Encouraging Videos* — Look for videos or stories that teach you more about following Jesus!

what's next

discussion questions

1. What are some ways you can use technology to help you grow closer to God?
2. Have you ever listened to a song or video that helped you feel connected to God?
3. How can you make time for God, even when there are lots of fun things to do online?

let's pray

Dear God, thank You for tools like music and apps that help me learn about You. Help me to use technology in ways that draw me closer to You. Show me how to make space for You every day. In Jesus name, we pray. Amen.

use tech the right way.

today i'm grateful for:

1. _____

2. _____

3. _____

today i learned that: _____

_____

_____

_____

my thoughts for the day: _____

_____

_____

_____

make a difference anywhere.

Read: James 1:22

Have you ever heard great advice but forgot to follow it?

What happened:

It's easy to listen to good advice but forget to follow it.

The same thing can happen with our faith. We might hear a great Bible verse or go to church and feel inspired, but then we go back to our regular day and forget to live it out.

The Bible tells us in James 1:22, *"Do not merely listen to the word, and so deceive yourselves. Do what it says."*

That means our faith isn't just something we hear about; it's something we **live out!** This is true both offline and online.

It's great to post positive things, but your actions matter even more. Being kind online is important. But are you also being kind in real life? Encouraging your friends at school? Helping your family at home?

When your online actions and your real-life choices match, people see that your faith is real.

You make a difference not just with what you post, but with how you treat people every single day.

Living Out Your Faith Everywhere:

1. *Be Kind Online and Offline* — Make sure your kindness isn't just for the screen.
2. *Follow Through on Good Ideas* — If you read something encouraging, find a way to live it out today!
3. *Be the Same Person Everywhere* — Let your actions match your words, both in what you post and how you treat people in real life.

what's next

discussion questions

1. Why is it important for your online actions and your real-life actions to match?
2. What does it look like to live out your faith, not just talk about it?
3. Can you think of one way to show kindness both online and offline this week?

let's pray

Dear God, help me to live out my faith in everything I do. Let my actions and words match, and let people see Your love in how I treat them. Help me make a difference wherever I am. In Jesus name, we pray. Amen.

be the same person everywhere.

today i'm grateful for:

1. _____

2. _____

3. _____

today i learned that: _____

_____

_____

_____

my thoughts for the day: _____

_____

_____

_____

conclusion

conclusion

As we wrap up our journey together, it's incredible to see how far you've come and how much you've learned.

WEEK ONE reminded you that your worth is not found in likes, followers, or what others think. Your value is found in who God created you to be; fearfully and wonderfully made.

WEEK TWO challenged you to guard your heart and mind by choosing wisely what you watch, believe, and click. What you let in shapes who you are becoming.

WEEK THREE showed you the unbelievable power your words have to bring life, to build others up, and to shine hope in a world that really needs it.

WEEK FOUR called you to live out your faith everywhere; in your words, your posts, your actions, both online and offline. Every choice you make is a chance to reflect the love of Jesus.

We may not have covered every situation you'll face.

We may not have answered every question that will come your way.

But you now have truth to stand on, tools to use, and the confidence that you are never walking through this alone.

So this week...

Stand tall in who God says you are.
Choose what builds you up.
Use your words to lift others higher.
Live your faith out loud.

And never forget, when you live with kindness, truth, and love, you are shining the light of Jesus to a world that needs it!

author bio

JOSHUA CELESTIN gives leadership to 4th & 5th graders at his local church in Orlando, which means he spends every day thinking about, speaking to, interacting with, and playing games with preteens, as well as recruiting leaders to work with them.

Before stepping into his current role, Josh spent five years as a filmmaker and is an Emmy award-winning cinematographer, dedicated to telling and sharing others' stories.

Josh did not limit himself to storytelling through film but extended his talents to Christian hip-hop as well.

Most importantly, Josh leads a small group of 5th graders every Sunday. If you want to be Josh's best friend, just buy him a pizza.

For more resources from Strong Series check out . . .

Start Strong Devotional:
a four week devotional for preteens exploring friends, choices, bullying & conflict.

SUPPORT FOR EVERY STEP

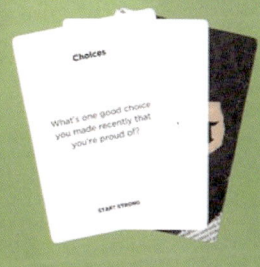

Leader Guide   **Icebreaker Cards**   **T-Shirt**

www.ingramcontent.com/pod-product-compliance
Lightning Source LLC
Chambersburg PA
CBRC090836120626
46551CB00007B/678